From (date)

To (date)

OWNER

Address

Phone

Email Address

NOTES

Credit Card Information

Credit Card Info	Name on Card	Number	Exp. Date	Code

Banking (Checking/Savings) Information

Account Type (Checking/Savings)	Name on Account	Account Number	Routing Number

NOTES

Online Account Information

Company	ID/Login	Password	Notes

Security ? #1	Security ? #2	Security ? #3	Security ? #4
Security Answer #1	Security Answer #2	Security Answer #3	Security Answer #4

Company	ID/Login	Password	Notes

Security ? #1	Security ? #2	Security ? #3	Security ? #4
Security Answer #1	Security Answer #2	Security Answer #3	Security Answer #4

Company	ID/Login	Password	Notes

Security ? #1	Security ? #2	Security ? #3	Security ? #4
Security Answer #1	Security Answer #2	Security Answer #3	Security Answer #4

Company	ID/Login	Password	Notes

Security ? #1	Security ? #2	Security ? #3	Security ? #4
Security Answer #1	Security Answer #2	Security Answer #3	Security Answer #4

Company	ID/Login	Password	Notes

Security ? #1	Security ? #2	Security ? #3	Security ? #4
Security Answer #1	Security Answer #2	Security Answer #3	Security Answer #4

Company	ID/Login	Password	Notes

Security ? #1	Security ? #2	Security ? #3	Security ? #4
Security Answer #1	Security Answer #2	Security Answer #3	Security Answer #4

Company	ID/Login	Password	Notes

Security ? #1	Security ? #2	Security ? #3	Security ? #4
Security Answer #1	Security Answer #2	Security Answer #3	Security Answer #4

Online Account Information

Company	ID/Login	Password	Notes

Security ? #1	Security ? #2	Security ? #3	Security ? #4
Security Answer #1	Security Answer #2	Security Answer #3	Security Answer #4

Company	ID/Login	Password	Notes

Security ? #1	Security ? #2	Security ? #3	Security ? #4
Security Answer #1	Security Answer #2	Security Answer #3	Security Answer #4

Company	ID/Login	Password	Notes

Security ? #1	Security ? #2	Security ? #3	Security ? #4
Security Answer #1	Security Answer #2	Security Answer #3	Security Answer #4

Company	ID/Login	Password	Notes

Security ? #1	Security ? #2	Security ? #3	Security ? #4
Security Answer #1	Security Answer #2	Security Answer #3	Security Answer #4

Company	ID/Login	Password	Notes

Security ? #1	Security ? #2	Security ? #3	Security ? #4
Security Answer #1	Security Answer #2	Security Answer #3	Security Answer #4

Company	ID/Login	Password	Notes

Security ? #1	Security ? #2	Security ? #3	Security ? #4
Security Answer #1	Security Answer #2	Security Answer #3	Security Answer #4

Company	ID/Login	Password	Notes

Security ? #1	Security ? #2	Security ? #3	Security ? #4
Security Answer #1	Security Answer #2	Security Answer #3	Security Answer #4

Online Account Information

Company	ID/Login	Password	Notes

Security ? #1	Security ? #2	Security ? #3	Security ? #4
Security Answer #1	Security Answer #2	Security Answer #3	Security Answer #4

Company	ID/Login	Password	Notes

Security ? #1	Security ? #2	Security ? #3	Security ? #4
Security Answer #1	Security Answer #2	Security Answer #3	Security Answer #4

Company	ID/Login	Password	Notes

Security ? #1	Security ? #2	Security ? #3	Security ? #4
Security Answer #1	Security Answer #2	Security Answer #3	Security Answer #4

Company	ID/Login	Password	Notes

Security ? #1	Security ? #2	Security ? #3	Security ? #4
Security Answer #1	Security Answer #2	Security Answer #3	Security Answer #4

Company	ID/Login	Password	Notes

Security ? #1	Security ? #2	Security ? #3	Security ? #4
Security Answer #1	Security Answer #2	Security Answer #3	Security Answer #4

Company	ID/Login	Password	Notes

Security ? #1	Security ? #2	Security ? #3	Security ? #4
Security Answer #1	Security Answer #2	Security Answer #3	Security Answer #4

Company	ID/Login	Password	Notes

Security ? #1	Security ? #2	Security ? #3	Security ? #4
Security Answer #1	Security Answer #2	Security Answer #3	Security Answer #4

Online Account Information

Company	ID/Login	Password	Notes

Security ? #1	Security ? #2	Security ? #3	Security ? #4
Security Answer #1	Security Answer #2	Security Answer #3	Security Answer #4

Company	ID/Login	Password	Notes

Security ? #1	Security ? #2	Security ? #3	Security ? #4
Security Answer #1	Security Answer #2	Security Answer #3	Security Answer #4

Company	ID/Login	Password	Notes

Security ? #1	Security ? #2	Security ? #3	Security ? #4
Security Answer #1	Security Answer #2	Security Answer #3	Security Answer #4

Company	ID/Login	Password	Notes

Security ? #1	Security ? #2	Security ? #3	Security ? #4
Security Answer #1	Security Answer #2	Security Answer #3	Security Answer #4

Company	ID/Login	Password	Notes

Security ? #1	Security ? #2	Security ? #3	Security ? #4
Security Answer #1	Security Answer #2	Security Answer #3	Security Answer #4

Company	ID/Login	Password	Notes

Security ? #1	Security ? #2	Security ? #3	Security ? #4
Security Answer #1	Security Answer #2	Security Answer #3	Security Answer #4

Company	ID/Login	Password	Notes

Security ? #1	Security ? #2	Security ? #3	Security ? #4
Security Answer #1	Security Answer #2	Security Answer #3	Security Answer #4

JANURY _____

Due Date	Bill Description	Amount Due	Amount Paid	Paid Date	Confirmation Number	Notes

Notes for the Month

_____

_____

_____

_____

_____

_____

_____

_____

_____

_____

_____

NOTES

February _____

Due Date	Bill Description	Amount Due	Amount Paid	Paid Date	Confirmation Number	Notes

Notes for the Month

_____
_____
_____
_____
_____
_____
_____
_____
_____
_____

NOTES

March _____

Due Date	Bill Description	Amount Due	Amount Paid	Paid Date	Confirmation Number	Notes

Notes for the Month

_____
_____
_____
_____
_____
_____
_____
_____
_____
_____
_____

NOTES

April _____

Due Date	Bill Description	Amount Due	Amount Paid	Paid Date	Confirmation Number	Notes

Notes for the Month

_____
_____
_____
_____
_____
_____
_____
_____
_____
_____
_____

NOTES

May _____

Due Date	Bill Description	Amount Due	Amount Paid	Paid Date	Confirmation Number	Notes

Notes for the Month

_____
_____
_____
_____
_____
_____
_____
_____
_____
_____
_____

NOTES

June _____

Due Date	Bill Description	Amount Due	Amount Paid	Paid Date	Confirmation Number	Notes

Notes for the Month

NOTES

July _____

Due Date	Bill Description	Amount Due	Amount Paid	Paid Date	Confirmation Number	Notes

Notes for the Month

_____
_____
_____
_____
_____
_____
_____
_____
_____
_____
_____
_____

NOTES

August _____

Due Date	Bill Description	Amount Due	Amount Paid	Paid Date	Confirmation Number	Notes

Notes for the Month

_____
_____
_____
_____
_____
_____
_____
_____
_____
_____

NOTES

September _____

Due Date	Bill Description	Amount Due	Amount Paid	Paid Date	Confirmation Number	Notes

Notes for the Month

_____
_____
_____
_____
_____
_____
_____
_____
_____
_____
_____

October _____

Due Date	Bill Description	Amount Due	Amount Paid	Paid Date	Confirmation Number	Notes

Notes for the Month

_____
_____
_____
_____
_____
_____
_____
_____
_____
_____
_____

NOTES

November _____

Due Date	Bill Description	Amount Due	Amount Paid	Paid Date	Confirmation Number	Notes

Notes for the Month

NOTES

December _____

Due Date	Bill Description	Amount Due	Amount Paid	Paid Date	Confirmation Number	Notes

Notes for the Month

_____

_____

_____

_____

_____

_____

_____

_____

_____

_____

_____

NOTES

JANUARY _____

Due Date	Bill Description	Amount Due	Amount Paid	Paid Date	Confirmation Number	Notes

Notes for the Month

_____
_____
_____
_____
_____
_____
_____
_____
_____
_____

NOTES

February _____

Due Date	Bill Description	Amount Due	Amount Paid	Paid Date	Confirmation Number	Notes

Notes for the Month

NOTES

March _____

Due Date	Bill Description	Amount Due	Amount Paid	Paid Date	Confirmation Number	Notes

Notes for the Month

_____
_____
_____
_____
_____
_____
_____
_____
_____
_____
_____

NOTES

April _____

Due Date	Bill Description	Amount Due	Amount Paid	Paid Date	Confirmation Number	Notes

Notes for the Month

_____
_____
_____
_____
_____
_____
_____
_____
_____
_____
_____

NOTES

May _____

Due Date	Bill Description	Amount Due	Amount Paid	Paid Date	Confirmation Number	Notes

Notes for the Month

NOTES

June _____

Due Date	Bill Description	Amount Due	Amount Paid	Paid Date	Confirmation Number	Notes

Notes for the Month

_____
_____
_____
_____
_____
_____
_____
_____
_____
_____

NOTES

July _____

Due Date	Bill Description	Amount Due	Amount Paid	Paid Date	Confirmation Number	Notes

Notes for the Month

NOTES

August _____

Due Date	Bill Description	Amount Due	Amount Paid	Paid Date	Confirmation Number	Notes

Notes for the Month

_____

_____

_____

_____

_____

_____

_____

_____

_____

_____

_____

NOTES

September _____

Due Date	Bill Description	Amount Due	Amount Paid	Paid Date	Confirmation Number	Notes

Notes for the Month

NOTES

October _____

Due Date	Bill Description	Amount Due	Amount Paid	Paid Date	Confirmation Number	Notes

Notes for the Month

NOTES

November _____

Due Date	Bill Description	Amount Due	Amount Paid	Paid Date	Confirmation Number	Notes

Notes for the Month

_____
_____
_____
_____
_____
_____
_____
_____
_____
_____
_____

NOTES

December _____

Due Date	Bill Description	Amount Due	Amount Paid	Paid Date	Confirmation Number	Notes

Notes for the Month

_____

_____

_____

_____

_____

_____

_____

_____

_____

NOTES

JANUARY _____

Due Date	Bill Description	Amount Due	Amount Paid	Paid Date	Confirmation Number	Notes

Notes for the Month

_____
_____
_____
_____
_____
_____
_____
_____
_____
_____
_____

NOTES

February _____

Due Date	Bill Description	Amount Due	Amount Paid	Paid Date	Confirmation Number	Notes

Notes for the Month

_____

_____

_____

_____

_____

_____

_____

_____

_____

NOTES

March _____

Due Date	Bill Description	Amount Due	Amount Paid	Paid Date	Confirmation Number	Notes

Notes for the Month

NOTES

April _____

Due Date	Bill Description	Amount Due	Amount Paid	Paid Date	Confirmation Number	Notes

Notes for the Month

_____

_____

_____

_____

_____

_____

_____

_____

_____

_____

_____

May _____

Due Date	Bill Description	Amount Due	Amount Paid	Paid Date	Confirmation Number	Notes

Notes for the Month

NOTES

June _____

Due Date	Bill Description	Amount Due	Amount Paid	Paid Date	Confirmation Number	Notes

Notes for the Month

NOTES

July _____

Due Date	Bill Description	Amount Due	Amount Paid	Paid Date	Confirmation Number	Notes

Notes for the Month

_____

_____

_____

_____

_____

_____

_____

_____

_____

_____

_____

NOTES

August _____

Due Date	Bill Description	Amount Due	Amount Paid	Paid Date	Confirmation Number	Notes

Notes for the Month

_____
_____
_____
_____
_____
_____
_____
_____
_____
_____
_____
_____
_____

NOTES

September _____

Due Date	Bill Description	Amount Due	Amount Paid	Paid Date	Confirmation Number	Notes

Notes for the Month

NOTES

October _____

Due Date	Bill Description	Amount Due	Amount Paid	Paid Date	Confirmation Number	Notes

Notes for the Month

_____
_____
_____
_____
_____
_____
_____
_____
_____
_____
_____

NOTES

November _____

Due Date	Bill Description	Amount Due	Amount Paid	Paid Date	Confirmation Number	Notes

Notes for the Month

_____
_____
_____
_____
_____
_____
_____
_____
_____
_____
_____

NOTES

December _____

Due Date	Bill Description	Amount Due	Amount Paid	Paid Date	Confirmation Number	Notes

Notes for the Month

_____
_____
_____
_____
_____
_____
_____
_____
_____
_____
_____

NOTES

JANUARY _____

Due Date	Bill Description	Amount Due	Amount Paid	Paid Date	Confirmation Number	Notes

Notes for the Month

_____
_____
_____
_____
_____
_____
_____
_____
_____
_____
_____

NOTES

February _____

Due Date	Bill Description	Amount Due	Amount Paid	Paid Date	Confirmation Number	Notes

Notes for the Month

_____
_____
_____
_____
_____
_____
_____
_____
_____
_____
_____

NOTES

March _____

Due Date	Bill Description	Amount Due	Amount Paid	Paid Date	Confirmation Number	Notes

Notes for the Month

_____
_____
_____
_____
_____
_____
_____
_____
_____
_____
_____

NOTES

April _____

Due Date	Bill Description	Amount Due	Amount Paid	Paid Date	Confirmation Number	Notes

Notes for the Month

NOTES

May _____

Due Date	Bill Description	Amount Due	Amount Paid	Paid Date	Confirmation Number	Notes

Notes for the Month

_____
_____
_____
_____
_____
_____
_____
_____
_____
_____
_____

NOTES

June _____

Due Date	Bill Description	Amount Due	Amount Paid	Paid Date	Confirmation Number	Notes

Notes for the Month

NOTES

July _____

Due Date	Bill Description	Amount Due	Amount Paid	Paid Date	Confirmation Number	Notes

Notes for the Month

_____
_____
_____
_____
_____
_____
_____
_____
_____
_____
_____

NOTES

August _____

Due Date	Bill Description	Amount Due	Amount Paid	Paid Date	Confirmation Number	Notes

Notes for the Month

NOTES

September _____

Due Date	Bill Description	Amount Due	Amount Paid	Paid Date	Confirmation Number	Notes

Notes for the Month

_____
_____
_____
_____
_____
_____
_____
_____
_____
_____
_____
_____

NOTES

October _____

Due Date	Bill Description	Amount Due	Amount Paid	Paid Date	Confirmation Number	Notes

Notes for the Month

NOTES

November _____

Due Date	Bill Description	Amount Due	Amount Paid	Paid Date	Confirmation Number	Notes

Notes for the Month

NOTES

December _____

Due Date	Bill Description	Amount Due	Amount Paid	Paid Date	Confirmation Number	Notes

Notes for the Month

NOTES

JANUARY _____

Due Date	Bill Description	Amount Due	Amount Paid	Paid Date	Confirmation Number	Notes

Notes for the Month

_____
_____
_____
_____
_____
_____
_____
_____
_____
_____
_____

NOTES

February _____

Due Date	Bill Description	Amount Due	Amount Paid	Paid Date	Confirmation Number	Notes

Notes for the Month

_____
_____
_____
_____
_____
_____
_____
_____
_____
_____
_____

NOTES

March _____

Due Date	Bill Description	Amount Due	Amount Paid	Paid Date	Confirmation Number	Notes

Notes for the Month

_____
_____
_____
_____
_____
_____
_____
_____
_____
_____

NOTES

April _____

Due Date	Bill Description	Amount Due	Amount Paid	Paid Date	Confirmation Number	Notes

Notes for the Month

NOTES

May _____

Due Date	Bill Description	Amount Due	Amount Paid	Paid Date	Confirmation Number	Notes

Notes for the Month

NOTES

June _____

Due Date	Bill Description	Amount Due	Amount Paid	Paid Date	Confirmation Number	Notes

Notes for the Month

_____
_____
_____
_____
_____
_____
_____
_____
_____
_____

NOTES

July _____

Due Date	Bill Description	Amount Due	Amount Paid	Paid Date	Confirmation Number	Notes

Notes for the Month

_____

_____

_____

_____

_____

_____

_____

_____

_____

_____

_____

NOTES

August _____

Due Date	Bill Description	Amount Due	Amount Paid	Paid Date	Confirmation Number	Notes

Notes for the Month

_____
_____
_____
_____
_____
_____
_____
_____
_____
_____
_____

NOTES

September _____

Due Date	Bill Description	Amount Due	Amount Paid	Paid Date	Confirmation Number	Notes

Notes for the Month

NOTES

October _____

Due Date	Bill Description	Amount Due	Amount Paid	Paid Date	Confirmation Number	Notes

Notes for the Month

NOTES

November _____

Due Date	Bill Description	Amount Due	Amount Paid	Paid Date	Confirmation Number	Notes

Notes for the Month

_____
_____
_____
_____
_____
_____
_____
_____
_____

NOTES

December _____

Due Date	Bill Description	Amount Due	Amount Paid	Paid Date	Confirmation Number	Notes

Notes for the Month

NOTES

NOTES

NOTES